A City Girl With A Broken Heart

A Collection of Poems

Zuleyma Guerrero

BookLeaf Publishing
India | USA | UK

Made with ❤ on the BookLeaf Publishing Platform
www.bookleafpub.in
www.bookleafpub.com

Dedication

Elizabeth, Tayna, Anyelo and Chip

Thank you!

I wouldn't be me, if you weren't you.

Preface

Acknowledgements

Love Peace, But Understand War

When hope flickers dim,
Yet embers still glow,
When you dance with shadows,
But seek the light's flow.

When you gather your dreams,
Yet they drift far away,
When you cherish the silence,
But hear chaos at play.

When you breathe in the calm,
Yet storms start to roar,
When you love peace,
But understand war.

Butterflies, To Snake Vibes

From giving me butterflies
To snake vibes,
When did things change
Not that I expect, them to
Always be the same
No more hugs & kisses
Saying goodbye to
Being your Misses
The future isn't clear,
When you aren't near
A new me, will rise
Completing all my dreams,
From the night
I will soar, I will fly,
Reaching for stars, forgetting the why,
With strength in my heart, I'll reclaim my air,
A woman reborn, shedding despair.
In the quiet of dawn, I'll find my way,
A journey of hope, come what may.

Thoughts Of You

So I hold onto whispers, the warmth of your touch,
In memories woven, I cherish so much.
Thoughts of you cloud my mind,
Like all the time.
Remembering the things that used to be
Come so naturally to me
I miss the way your lips
Always found a kiss
Telling me of all the beauty
In the world
And how I'm your favorite girl
Things are different, things have changed
Seems like nothing is the same
Yet in this silence, echoes grow louder,
Moments linger, I can't help but ponder.
Through shadows cast, your light I seek,
In dreams we meet, as hearts still speak.
Though distance may stretch like the evening sky,
In the depths of my heart, you never say goodbye.

You Think I Don't Know

You think I don’t know
That secrets creep and crawl
Behind each careless lie,
As shadows on your wall.
You think I don’t know
How you glance at your phone,
Wishing for a past, that feels like home,
Caught between the laughter,
And the tears you won't show.
You think I don’t know
That love shouldn’t feel
Like a game of hide and seek,
But here I am,
Heart in my hand,
Wanting to understand.
You think I don’t know
But deep down I see,
The truth that lingers
Unfolding silently.
Yet still I stay, hoping for a sign,

That this love will be ours,
And you'll finally choose,
To be mine.

Lonely Me

I'm so lonely,
But I'm still running from me,
Scared to know what's beneath
The pain, the tears, the lies
So sick of wondering why
Things happen like they do
And nothing seems to move
Chasing sunsets, waves and beaches
Are nice
But what happens at night time
When it's too dark to see
& I'm just left with me
In shadows that whisper,
Secrets I can't bear to keep,
Echoes of dreams undone,
In silence, my heart weeps.
The mirror shows a ghost,
Familiar yet so strange,
Fighting through the stillness,
Longing for a change.

Morning Rays

Sometimes missing you,
Keeps me up at night
Then all of a sudden
I'm happy to be alive,
Feeling all these emotions,
Lets me know I'm ok.
Life is nothing but a maze
Twist and turns, ups and downs
Life is a merry go round
Have some fun, have some laughs
You will notice the pain
Doesn't last.
And though the shadows creep,
They melt with morning's ease.
And in this dance of highs and lows,
I find my spirit warm.
In this tapestry of life I weave,
Love's thread is never dead.

I Miss You

Missing you doesn't feel right,
You're all I think about at night
How sweet were your kisses
Me being your future Mrs.
But something changed, and
Nothing is the same
Feels like being left at sea
And it's just me
The thoughts come in
As waves
Something I can't explain
I search for solace, but it's late
Drifting through shadows of what used to be
In a silent storm, it's just me
With memories crashing, pulling me down
In this ocean of heartache, I'm bound
Yet hope flickers like a distant light,
Perhaps one day, love will take flight.

Sometimes People, People Sometimes

Sometimes people laugh
Sometimes people cry
Sometimes people dance
Sometimes people sigh
Sometimes people heal
Sometimes people ache
Sometimes people dream
Sometimes people wake
Sometimes people hope
Sometimes people fear
Sometimes people love
Sometimes people near
Sometimes people
People Sometimes

Today

But today, nothing is the same
Can't even look at your face
It brings tears to my eyes
Really makes me want to cry
Because now you're acting brand new
It's like I don't even know you
So today we say goodbye
You're no longer mine.

I'll take back my heart, reclaim my soul,
Found strength in the silence, now I'm whole.
You were a chapter, but now I turn the page,
Embracing the beauty of my newfound stage.

My Guy

Not a care in the world,
Just being a regular girl
Happy with my guy, he's all mine
Sun shining on my face,
There's nothing I would replace
With birds soaring over me
It's so beautiful, just to be
Over the hill, chasing your feet
New experiences, we meet
The first one to the top
Hoping this feeling
Never stops, make this last forever
It simply couldn't get, better.
With laughter echoing wide,
Together we'll take it all in stride,
Holding hands as day turns to night,
Under the stars, whispers shared,
In this bliss, we know we dared.
A lifetime packed in sunlit hours,
Life unfolds like blooming flowers.

Will You?

Late at night,
I stare up at the moon, and
Wonder if it's you, who,
Will keep me safe
Help me take the pain away
Watch me cry,
With no judgment why,
And in the silence between breaths,
Where our whispers linger low,
Guide me through the shadows,
Let your heart be my home,
Together we'll find solace,
In the darkness, a glow,
Unraveling the threads,
Of a love yet unknown.

Little Girl

It’s exhausting,
Trying to hide,
All the parts of me
I think you don’t want to see
The things that truly make me,
Unique
The truths I believe about the world
The lies I was told as a little girl
Yet here I stand, on this fragile ground,
Wrestling shadows, silent, profound,
If I laid bare my heart's intricate design,
Would you embrace the chaos, or draw the line?

I Love You

I love you
Like the waves kiss the shore
Their rhythm a dance, forevermore
I love you
Like the whispers of the trees
Swaying gently in the evening breeze
I love you
Like the sun warms the earth
Filling every moment with vibrance and mirth
I love you
Like the heartbeat in my chest
A promise of love that will never rest
I love you
Like the dawn chases the night
Bringing forth hope, in its soft light
I love you
With every breath I take
In this life's journey, together we'll make.

Let's Create

With dreams as our canvas,
Let's paint with bold hues,
Crafting moments,
Chasing the light that ensues.

Let whispers of hope
Guide us through the night,
With hands intertwined,
We'll dare to ignite.

With visions unspoken,
We'll dance in the glow,
In colors that shimmer,
Where wild passions flow.

Through shadows and echoes,
We'll carve out our space,
With hearts ever open,
We'll find our embrace.

Search And You Shall Find

I wandered through shadows, a ghost in the flame,
Searching for echoes of a once vibrant name.
In corners of silence, where whispers retreat,
I discovered the remnants of love bittersweet.

I reached for the memories, now shifting like sand,
Grasping at moments I could no longer understand.
The laughter we shared wrapped in sorrow's embrace,
Now a haunting refrain that time cannot erase.

But through the heartache, a glimmer resides,
A flicker of hope where true longing abides.
For though I've lost much, this journey's not done,
In searching for solace, I might find the sun.

Dance With Me

So madly in love with you
I see you in my dreams
Even though that's not where
You should be
If I had one wish
I'll be in your arms
From sunrise to dawn
As moonlight whispers
Secrets only we can share
Each heartbeat a melody,
Echoing through the night,
With every breath a promise,
Our souls taking flight.
In the tender glow of twilight,
We'll dance in soft embrace,
Two hearts forever woven,
In this enchanted space.

June

Yet in the shadows where we stood,
Echoes of laughter, that whispering good,
Time may drift and seasons turn,
But for your warmth, my heart still yearns.

I miss the way your eyes would shine,
Lighting paths, intertwining our lines.
Though distance stretches, love's thread unwinds,
Thoughts of you, always here, never behind.

Through days and nights, though apart we roam,
In dreams, I find the comfort of home.
So even as the world rearranges,
Thoughts of you, my heart still exchanges.

A Careful Disguise

Can you accept, the shadows I cast,
The echoes of laughter, of joy and of past?
If only you'd see
The vibrant chaos inside,
Maybe then I could breathe,
And let my heart guide.
It's exhausting,
Trying to hide, all the parts of me
I think you don't want to see
The things that truly make me,
Unique
The truths I believe about the world
The lies I was told as a little girl
I wear a mask,
A careful disguise,
Crafted from whispers, and timid goodbyes.
Yet beneath the surface,
A fire still burns, longing for freedom,
From the lessons I've learned.

City Girl

New York City
The Place I call home
Where everyone is different
And its ok to roam
The people, the places
Literally everyone's dream
The perfect place just to be
In a tapestry woven with hope and schemes.
A symphony ringing in the bustling streets,
Where laughter and culture collide and meet.
Skyscrapers stretching like hands to the sky,
Embracing the chaos, breathing a sigh.
From dawn's gentle light to the glow of the night,
My city ignites with vibrant delight.

Not Mine

I love you
And I can't believe
That you really aren't meant for me
The thought sometimes
Makes me cry
Wonder why
The stars align
Yet our paths diverge,
Each whispered dream
A soft, silent urge.
In moonlit nights
Where shadows play,
I search for signs
To lead you my way.

Goodbye, Hello

I say goodbye and it makes me better
I couldn't be this way forever
I learned many lessons
That I will carry with me
Learning, but never defeat
Tomorrow the sun shines bright
No more needs to fight
I love myself more
This pain has hit its core
So I say goodbye to you
Loving me is the new due
With each step forward, I reclaim my heart,
From shadows past, I now depart.
The whispers of doubt no longer confine,
In the garden of strength, I bloom and shine.
So watch me soar, unchained and free,
For the greatest love story starts with me.